JESUS
THE KING

STUDY GUIDE

Ezekiel
38-39

JESUS
THE KING

EXPLORING THE LIFE AND DEATH OF
THE SON OF GOD

STUDY GUIDE

NINE SESSIONS

TIMOTHY KELLER
AND SPENCE SHELTON

ZONDERVAN

Jesus the King Study Guide
Copyright © 2015 by Redeemer City to City

This title is also available as a Zondervan ebook. Visit www.zondervan.com/ebooks.

Requests for information should be addressed to:

Zondervan, *3900 Sparks Dr. SE, Grand Rapids, Michigan 49546*

ISBN 978-0-310-81444-3

Interior design: Denise Froehlich

First Printing December 2014 / Printed in the United States of America

CONTENTS

INTRODUCTION

In the few years since the publication of *Jesus the King* (originally titled *King's Cross*), I've spoken to people who, in seeking to present and recommend Christianity to someone, prefer this book over another volume I wrote, *The Reason for God*. I agree. Christianity is Jesus Christ, in a way that Islam is not Muhammad, nor Buddhism Buddha. Other religions were founded by teachers who pointed to a body of truth, and a way to find life, but Jesus says "I am the Way, the Truth, and the Life." And so any book that simply summarizes the beliefs of Christianity cannot get us as close to the heart of it as a sustained look at Jesus himself.

I also believe that before many people will pay close attention to a case for why Christianity is true, they should first be brought to see why they might want it to be true. And there is no more rightful way to make Christianity deeply attractive than to display Jesus in all his wisdom, power, gentleness, and beauty. So ultimately I would say that this book and *Reason* are complementary. They need each other.

It is quite appropriate that this study guide should be written to facilitate group discussion of both *Jesus the King* and the Gospel of Mark. My book was based on a series of sermons preached on Sunday mornings at Redeemer Presbyterian Church in New York City during 2006 and 2007. However, long before that, I wrote a series of Bible studies that my wife and I used for several years to lead weekly discussion groups.

There we came to trust that the straightforward accounts of what Jesus said and did have a remarkable power to work upon people. We didn't have to lecture, expound, and expostulate at length. Indeed, we learned a lot as members of our groups pointed out things in the text we had not noticed. The later sermons were filled with insights from those experiences of learning about Jesus in community. People's lives changed as they came into contact with Jesus the King.

I'm delighted that through this study guide that kind of experience will become available to so many others. And I'm grateful to be collaborating with Spence Shelton, whose experience as a pastor and study author with a deep understanding of the real-world dynamics of the gospel make him an excellent guide to this book.

Tim Keller, November, 2014

HOW TO USE THIS STUDY GUIDE

Welcome to the *Jesus the King* small group experience. Over the course of nine sessions you will read through the entirety of Timothy Keller's book *Jesus the King* (Riverhead Books) as well as the full Gospel of Mark. Each of the nine sessions focuses on helping the group participants understand and apply one "big idea" brought out in *Jesus the King*.

---&asterism;---

Overview of the Session Format

Each session in this study guide is broken into three parts: *Pre-Group*, *Group Discussion*, and *On Your Own*. *Pre-Group* and *Group Discussion* are essential for a great group experience, while *On Your Own* is designed to help you dig further into the concepts if you so desire.

PRE-GROUP

(To be completed on your own prior to the group session)

Each session includes a Reading Assignment — a passage from the Gospel of Mark, chapters from the book *Jesus the King*, and the session Introduction — followed by a Personal Reflection assessment and a short set of Bible Investigation questions. Work through these before arriving at your group gathering so you can be prepared to share and learn from others.

GROUP DISCUSSION

(To be completed together during the group session)

This part of the session is to be done together with the other group members. You will review your Pre-Group work, then discuss and apply the key truths and ideas for the rest of the session. The group leader will facilitate this part, which is designed to be a thought-provoking, fun, interactive time together.

ON YOUR OWN

(To be completed individually after the group session)

The *On Your Own* section is an optional individual challenge to help you engage and apply your learning after the group gathering.

CALLED BY THE KING

Mark 1:1–20

———◦◦◦———

Pre-Group

Work through the following readings, Personal Reflection assessment, and Bible Investigation questions to prepare for the group gathering.

READING ASSIGNMENT

Mark 1:1–20 and chapters "Before," 1, and 2 of *Jesus the King* by Timothy Keller

INTRODUCTION

THE BIG IDEA

The gospel is not good advice; it's a summons to follow a king.

THE CALL TO REPENT AND BELIEVE

"The time is fulfilled, and the kingdom of God is at hand; repent and believe in the gospel." (Mark 1:15 ESV)

The first words Mark records from Jesus' mouth, "The time is fulfilled, and the kingdom of God is at hand," define the message and actions that will unfold in the rest of the book. Jesus bursts onto the scene not with a new code of ethics but with a news bulletin about a new reality.

That's why Jesus calls his message "gospel," which literally means "good news." In Jesus' day, this was not just any daily news but life-altering news. A "gospel" was so important it would hold the front pages of the news outlets for weeks. Whatever Jesus is declaring demands our full attention, and Mark reinforces this by putting it front and center: "The kingdom of God is at hand." Mark builds the body of his whole story from this headline. Every move Jesus makes, as recorded by Mark, illustrates for his readers that the kingdom of God—a new regime of perfect, healing leadership over the world—is near. Jesus' healings, his exorcisms, his mercy, his miracles, his authority over nature, his sacrifice, and his defeat of death are all filling out the story of this kingdom Jesus is announcing.

The Gospel of Mark's power lies in its simplicity and directness. It is a refreshing and powerful breaking news item to those of us who live in a sea of lifestyle guides. Think of the difference between news and advice. Advice is counsel on how to improve your life. "You should try yoga" or "Don't go to the one on 21st Street" or "You shouldn't vaccinate your kids" are all examples of advice. News, however, is not there to improve your life; news is there to tell you what has happened and its significance for you now that you've heard it. Whether you choose to believe a news story is entirely your prerogative, but if it is true, then to ignore it will have practical repercussions.

For example, when the research linking sun exposure and skin cancer confronts the average beach vacationer, one can change his or her normal routine via sunscreens and umbrellas, or carry on as normal. Both reactions—changing the routine or keeping it—are decisions on how to deal with the news about the effects of sun exposure.

The bigger and more personally relevant the news, the more deeply it challenges us. Because this news is about God as the King of the world and his vision for our lives, to believe it will be to repent of (literally, to turn away from) some of the basic premises we've built our lives on. If this gospel—that the kingdom of God is at hand, that Jesus is its King, and that he has earned our way to God—is true, it changes everything for us. Jesus says that to believe it will change us so foundationally that our work, our families, our ambitions—everything!—will change as well. We cannot simply add this message to the collection of convenient wisdom guiding our lives. Instead we will lose our lives as we know them for something better than we could ever have imagined.

THE CALL TO FOLLOW THE KING

At once they left their nets and followed him. (Mark 1:18)

To believe Jesus' news will be to believe he is your King. This grabs our attention, because most reading this have never lived under the rule of a king. The idea of one person having total rule over everything in society is difficult enough, but Jesus doesn't stop there. He claims immediate authority over *your* life specifically.

It may be difficult to put yourself into the scene with the disciples gripping their drenched, fishy-smelling nets. But remember that fishing has likely been their families' livelihood for generations. Jesus is a stanger, walking into their workplace, telling them they need to leave their family business and follow him on the spot. Here you begin to experience the disruptive nature of Jesus' kingship that Mark wants you to feel. "Follow me" is a big statement.

At this point, Mark is scant on the content of the message because he wants us to see the authority of the messenger. When the one calling me reveals himself to be not just any king but *my King*, I am left with little choice but to obey him then and there. When I find out following him will fulfill everything I've looked for in life, his once disruptive command is now my source of joy. I follow this King not only because I have to, but because following him gives me true meaning and joy.

This King's good news—that you do not need to earn your way to God—is so far-reaching that it is certain to disrupt your life. The good news—that out of his grace Jesus has made a way for you to come to God—frees you from the tyranny of having to build your own life résumé to impress God.

PERSONAL REFLECTION

An important part of any learning process is self-assessment: to determine where you are in relationship to the material presented. The point of the Personal Reflection section is not to feel good or bad about yourself but to help you visualize how the ideas in this session could affect your life. This assessment is situated prior to the Bible Investigation section so you can be aware of your own thinking as you begin studying Scripture. On a scale of 1–5 (1 = strongly disagree and 5 = strongly agree), select the number that best represents your response to each of the following statements.

If surveyed in an anonymous poll about religion, I would identify myself as a Christian.

(strongly disagree)   1   2   3   4   5   (strongly agree)

I feel comfortable when a conversation among friends shifts to religion and faith.

(strongly disagree)   1   2   3   4   5   (strongly agree)

I believe I understand what it means to actively, willingly relinquish authority of my life to Jesus.

(strongly disagree)   1   2   3   4   5   (strongly agree)

I am actively, willingly relinquishing authority of my entire life to Jesus.

(strongly disagree)   1   2   3   4   5   (strongly agree)

BIBLE INVESTIGATION

The following questions are designed to help you understand what is going on in the selected Bible passage. Write down your best responses, and try to avoid reading what others have said about the passage until after you've completed this section on your own. *(An occasional study help, "Go Deeper," appears throughout the study guide.)*

1. Mark opens his account with a reference to an Old Testament passage. Read Isaiah 40:3, and then compare it to Mark 1:1–4. What is Mark claiming about the identity of Jesus?

GO DEEPER: Mark is quoting a passage talking about Israel's God. Isaiah 40:3 uses the holy name only ascribed to God himself. By quoting a verse about Jesus' coming, Mark is emphatically claiming that Jesus is the God of Israel that Isaiah was talking about. By connecting the work of John the Baptist to the prophecy of Isaiah 40:3, Mark is unambiguous that Jesus is our God who has come.

---

2. Mark introduces readers to several characters in 1:9–13. List these characters and give any *brief* description (a phrase or a couple of words) from the Bible you may know about them.

3. What is the significance of Mark including these scenes (the baptism and the temptation of Jesus) with so many supernatural forces at play?

4. Verses 14–15 include Mark's first recorded words of Jesus, which set the trajectory for the rest of his book. What authority is Jesus claiming, and how does this claim inform the way you are to read the rest of the story? *(Read Colossians 1:15–20 for more help.)*

5. Having announced that the kingdom is at hand, Jesus calls his hearers to repentance and belief. Repentance is different than simply saying, "I'm sorry"—it means to completely turn away from something. So what does Jesus mean by repentance here?

6. Why does Jesus say to repent *and* believe instead of just *believe*?

7. What do you think Mark wants us as his readers to believe about Jesus through the response of the fishermen to Jesus' call?

—◦◦✦◦◦—

Group Discussion

After a time of welcome and opening prayer, spend a few minutes reviewing the Pre-Group study together (observations, questions, insights), and then jump into this session's application questions and group exercise.

REVIEW

1. In one sentence, how would you summarize Mark 1:1–20?

2. Look over your notes from the Pre-Group study. What stood out to you as the key point?

3. Which Bible Investigation questions, if any, did you have difficulty with or want to discuss further?

APPLICATION

These questions are designed to help you take the core ideas from the Pre-Group Study and introduce them into your own story.

4. Mark sets Jesus up as both God and King in the opening chapter. At this point in your story, do you believe this claim? *(Don't worry, this is only week one. The idea here is to honestly assess where you are spiritually right now, giving you something to look back to as you go through the study.)*

> The gospel isn't advice: It's the good news that you don't need to earn your way to God; Jesus has already done it for you.
>
> *Jesus the King*, p. 22

5. The gospel news is the core of the Christian faith, and yet Christianity often ends up cast as a set of behaviors, opinions, and positions. How have you viewed what it means to be a Christian up to this point? What "Christian behaviors" are you most inclined to feel proud of yourself for?

> "Follow me because I'm the King you've been looking for. Follow me because I have authority over everything, yet I have humbled myself for you. Because I died on the cross for you when you didn't have the right beliefs or the right behavior. Because I have brought you news, not advice. Because I'm your true love, your true life — follow me."
>
> *Jesus the King*, p. 24

6. Brainstorm together a short job description of a perfect king. Consider the king's key roles and responsibilities and how he relates to those under his authority.

7. The disciples left their lifelong careers immediately to follow Jesus. To submit to Jesus as King is no small step for anyone. What do you perceive as the biggest obstacles to you personally submitting to Jesus as King and transferring authority of your life over to him? If you already have submitted to Jesus as King, where in your life are you most likely to rebel against his authority?

8. What would your life look and feel like if you fully surrendered to this perfect King? Your work life? Love life? Family life? Financial life? Social life?

EXERCISE

Mark claims Jesus is God and King. Break into groups of two or three people and each write a list of one-word descriptors of who *you* understand Jesus to be, based on your personal experience as well as this study. After about five minutes, compare your lists with each other and discuss.

-
-
-
-
-
-
-

Feel free to share with the larger group any insight you learn from hearing each other's lists. Then close your time together in prayer.

—◆—

On Your Own

Reinforce and apply this session's learning by engaging in the Personal Challenge; then read ahead for next session.

PERSONAL CHALLENGE

The challenge is an individual exercise for you to complete at some point following this session but before the next, as a way to dig deeper into the application of the truths from this session.

The Gospel of Mark is the story of Jesus. On the next page, try writing down your own spiritual story this week. What are the high and low points in your story? Who are the main characters? For this particular exercise, keep it to 500 words or less. You will be coming back to this story in a later session.

READING ASSIGNMENT

Mark 2–3 and chapters 3–4 of *Jesus the King* by Timothy Keller

MY SPIRITUAL STORY

DEEPER HEALING

Mark 2:1–17

—⁓✦⁓—

Pre-Group

Work through the following readings, Personal Reflection assessment, and Bible Investigation questions to prepare for the group gathering.

READING ASSIGNMENT

Mark 2–3 and chapters 3–4 of *Jesus the King* by Timothy Keller

INTRODUCTION

THE BIG IDEA

There is one problem deeper than all of our other problems, and the key to healing this deepest problem is found in the gospel.

"THAT YOU MAY KNOW"

The band R.E.M. had a hit song in the early '90s called "Everybody Hurts," expressing the shared experience of pain across the human race. Whether it is caused by our own doing, by another person, or by forces beyond our control, everyone experiences pain. For many, healing that pain becomes a major life quest. Some men work their entire lives and conquer industries in hopes of somehow resolving the wounds they feel from an absent father in childhood. Others will try dozens of remedies for chronic physical pain that has plagued their bodies for years. In one way or another, we all hurt; and when we do, we all want relief from our pain.

In Mark 2 the man who couldn't walk surely wanted relief. We can reasonably guess that his friends did not climb atop a roof, cut a hole in it, and then bear his weight as they lowered him down through it . . . all *against* his will. The man wanted to walk. Perhaps this is why Mark gives us stories like these. We see our own affliction in the lame man and read ourselves into the story with Jesus. How many times have you prayed for God to ease your pain?

I (Spence) remember waking one night to find my wife undergoing what turned out to be a miscarriage. And throughout that night, as it became more clear that we would lose our child, I pleaded and begged God for healing. Like the lame man, on that day I didn't come to Jesus to hear 'Your sins are forgiven.' I came hoping for the miracle of 'Rise up!' In the moment of pain we all share the same cry: *God help me.*

Jesus looks on our pleas with the same compassion he looked on the plea of the lame man. And he has the same power to answer our cry for help. With the lame man he claimed to wield power that only God has, to offer healing that only God can offer. And in response to the skeptical onlookers he verified his claim by making the lame man able to walk.

A DEEPER HEALING

Mark includes this story that we may learn to exchange what we want for what God wants for us. In moments of pain we still want the sign, the physical healing, the relief. We want to get up and walk like the lame man. We may not see it, but in our pain there is also a deeper longing within us, for healing deeper than we know how to express. In this scene Jesus heals the man's body—a true blessing—so that we may believe he can also heal and forgive the soul. The man claiming to be God will suffer great pain so that our pain in this life will be eclipsed by a hope so great it swallows up the pain entirely.

PERSONAL REFLECTION

The point of the Personal Reflection section is not to feel good or bad about yourself, but to help you visualize how what you are learning could affect your life. This assessment is situated prior to the Bible Investigation section so you can be aware of your own thinking as you begin studying Scripture. On a scale of 1–5 (1 = strongly disagree and 5 = strongly agree), select the number that best represents your response to each of the following statements.

I sometimes wonder whether or not God cares about me.

        (strongly disagree)   1   2   3   4   5   (strongly agree)

I believe I need forgiveness from God.

        (strongly disagree)   1   2   3   4   5   (strongly agree)

The people closest to me would say I readily forgive others.

        (strongly disagree)   1   2   3   4   5   (strongly agree)

I am more likely to approach difficult circumstances with hope than with despair.

        (strongly disagree)   1   2   3   4   5   (strongly agree)

BIBLE INVESTIGATION

The following questions are designed to help you explore chapter 2 of Mark's Gospel. Take your time and write down your best response to each question.

1. Look at Mark 2:1–5. How would you characterize the "faith" that Jesus is responding to?

2. Why is Jesus' first response to the paralytic (v. 5) surprising to the various characters in the scene?

3. Why does Jesus forgive the paralytic?

4. Why does Jesus heal the paralytic?

GO DEEPER: Mark is reinforcing his thesis that Jesus is the Son of God by recounting Jesus' encounter with the lame man. This encounter took place in front of numerous witnesses, many of whom were Jews. Isaiah 35:6 says that when the Messiah comes, "Then will the lame leap like a deer." The healings of Jesus were not just acts of compassion but signals verifying that the prophecies about the Messiah were being fulfilled in Jesus. Why does Jesus forgive and heal the paralytic? Because Jesus wants to be very clear to his audience, and to us, that he is the one and only true God.

---

5. What is important about Mark's description of the crowd's response in verse 12?

6. What about the call Levi receives to follow Jesus (vv. 13–14) is similar to the previous story? What is different? What does this tell us about the call to follow Jesus?

7. What does Jesus mean by "righteous" and "sinners"? What is Jesus teaching his hearers through how he is using these terms?

8. Look back to Mark 1:40–45 and compare it with Mark 2:1–17. What theme binds this section of the Gospel of Mark together?

—◦◦✝◦◦—

Group Discussion

After a time of welcome and opening prayer, spend a few minutes reviewing your Pre-Group study together (observations, questions, insights), and then jump into this session's application questions and group exercise.

REVIEW

1. Open your Bible to Mark 2. Have one person summarize what happened in Mark 2:1–17.

2. What insights did you gather from the Bible Investigation section? What questions did your investigation leave unanswered?

3. What idea or insight did you find helpful in chapters 2–3 of *Jesus the King*?

APPLICATION

These questions are designed to help you take the core truths from the Introduction and the Bible Investigation sections and introduce them into your story. So that everyone can participate, consider dividing up into groups of two or three to respond to these questions.

4. What implications stand out to you from Mark 2:1–17 for how we are to live today?

> When the Bible talks about sin it is not just referring to the bad things we do. It's not just lying or lust or whatever the case may be — it is ignoring God in the world he has made; it's rebelling against him by living without reference to him.
>
> *Jesus the King*, p. 30

5. In what ways are you most likely to ignore God in your daily life? How would your life be different if you lived more "with reference to him"?

> You've distorted your deepest wish by trying to make it into your savior, and now that you finally have it, it's turned on you ... Jesus is not going to play the rotten practical joke of giving you your deepest wish — until he has shown you that it was for him all along.
>
> *Jesus the King*, pp. 32, 38

6. Describe a time when you experienced disappointment. You might recall a relationship or friendship that didn't work out as you had hoped, or something that you needed but didn't get (such as a job offer or physical healing). Or, conversely, you might recall a time you got something you wanted, but it didn't satisfy as you thought it would.

7. Why was forgiveness the paralytic's deepest need? Why is it our deepest need? What other "needs" do we feel are deeper than our need for forgiveness?

8. Just as Jesus had the power to heal the paralytic, he has the power to give you whatever you want. In light of Mark 2, how can you grow closer to God, instead of away from him, when he doesn't give you what you ask him for?

> If he not only heals this man but forgives his sins as well, he's taking a decisive, irreversible step down the path to his death. By taking that step, he is putting a down payment on our forgiveness.
>
> *Jesus the King*, p. 38

9. Jesus tells the Pharisees that he is only on earth to help people who realize how much they need God's help. Considering your current personal circumstances, how does this rebuke to the Pharisees encourage you? How does it caution you?

EXERCISE

Case Study: Brandon and Ashley are in their late twenties, married, with a two-year-old son. They are recent additions to your small group, having joined only two months ago, yet it seems like they are feeling "at home." Brandon confides in a couple of the guys that he hasn't had a job in a year, and last Thursday was turned down for yet another one. He says his failure to find a job is causing problems at home, as money is getting tighter—which is making his relationship with Ashley tenser. He believes they are three months from homelessness and thinks Ashley might leave with their son to go live with her mom until things "get better."

Using what you've learned from Mark 2:1–17 as a foundation, discuss how your group would care for Brandon and Ashley to provide hope and healing for them both. Then conclude the session with prayer.

—◦✦◦—

On Your Own

More deeply apply this session's truths by engaging in the Personal Challenge; then read ahead for next session.

PERSONAL CHALLENGE

The challenge is an individual exercise for you to complete at some point following this session but before the next, as a way to dig deeper into the application of the truths from this session.

One way we display our belief in the gospel is by forgiving others just as Christ has forgiven us (see Colossians 3:13). This challenge is designed to help you take a first step toward forgiving someone. Identify someone in your life who has hurt you in some way. Think and pray about what consequences you have experienced by not having forgiven them. Also in prayer, ask God for insight into any ways you may have contributed to them hurting you, or ways you may have hurt them in response to the betrayal. Using the space provided on the next page, compose a short letter (there are even ancient tools you can use called pen and paper) forgiving the person for what he or she did, clearly owning your offenses, but without excusing theirs. Try explaining your forgiveness in gospel language; for example, "I've found forgiveness in Christ for my sin, and that has freed me to be able to forgive others for things that I was holding onto."

Sending the letter is not a part of this challenge, but you may decide you want to do so. If you do, read back over it to ensure you are writing in a tone of humility and grace that models Christ, as opposed to judgment masked in "forgiveness" language.

You could also write this letter to someone you need to ask forgiveness from. In this case, you would explain your acknowledgment of the pain you caused as well as the forgiveness you've found in Christ. The goal of the letter is not to acquire the other person's forgiveness but to express your repentance.

READING ASSIGNMENT

Mark 4–5 and chapters 5–6 of *Jesus the King* by Timothy Keller

MORE THAN YOU EXPECTED

Mark 5:1–43

—◦◦✦◦◦—

Pre-Group

Work through the following readings, Personal Reflection assessment, and Bible Investigation questions to prepare for the group gathering.

READING ASSIGNMENT

Mark 4–5 and chapters 5–6 of *Jesus the King* by Timothy Keller

INTRODUCTION

THE BIG IDEA

If Jesus is who he said he is, we can trust him with everything—even the most broken areas of our lives.

HIS POWER IS GREATER

Who is this? Even the wind and the waves obey him!" Mark chapter 4 ends with the disciples sitting in a very small boat marveling in terror and wonder at Jesus, a man so powerful that he had just silenced a mammoth storm with a mere word. In chapter 5, Mark continues to document this power through three miraculous encounters, each exposing the authority and power of Jesus for three utterly different audiences. Mark gives us these three stories *together* because through them he wants to show us Jesus' consistent character.

These three people experience power far beyond their comprehension. The demons that tormented the Gerasene man knew as soon as they saw Jesus that he wielded the power of God. That is why this incoherent madman—who until this moment was so strong no one could subdue him—became a helpless beggar crumpled at the feet of Jesus. A woman stricken by a chronic illness found enough power—in Jesus' clothing alone—to heal her instantly and completely. And a mere whisper and touch of Jesus' hand defeated death. The power Jesus wields is far greater than anyone in these scenes expected. It is a power that we could only expect from God himself.

HIS MERCY RESTORES

These people are desperate for help, and Jesus is quick to extend a merciful hand. The woman, for instance, has had a discharge of blood for twelve years! She's spent all of her money looking for solutions, only to be right back where she began. Such defeat presses hopelessness deep. Yet though she is unclean and unfixable, Jesus' mercy is available to her. He reaches down almost instinctively and brings joy and restoration where there was only despair and brokenness. Speaking of despair, imagine Jairus when he receives word of his daughter's death, news so painful no father should ever have to hear it. Jesus gives compassion and mercy to him, and to his daughter, in bringing her back to life. The mercy of Jesus is available even to the man who has been "living" among the tombs. Where once there was bondage, shouting, and pain, Jesus restores sanity and health.

YOU CAN TRUST HIM

The key to Mark 5 is verse 36. Jesus meets Jairus in his most desperate moment and says, "Don't be afraid; just believe." For Jairus, to believe will mean to suspend all conventional wisdom about the devastating finality of death. Jesus knows that Jairus is about to careen right into grief and despair. But just as the news begins to load into Jairus's heart, Jesus jerks him back from the edge with a simple command: *Believe. Trust that I am who I say I am.* This is one of those statements that translates clearly through two thousand years of history right to you where you are today. Jairus came to Jesus expecting (or at least hoping for) healing. He didn't expect to go *through* the death of his daughter to see her well again. When you come to Jesus, you may not expect or even like where he takes you. But if you trust him, he will give you far more than you ever asked or imagined.

PERSONAL REFLECTION

On a scale of 1–5 (1 = strongly disagree and 5 = strongly agree), select the number that best represents your response to each of the following statements.

I believe God will provide for the current needs I have in my life.

(strongly disagree)   1   2   3   4   5   (strongly agree)

I have learned to be patient in waiting on God.

(strongly disagree)   1   2   3   4   5   (strongly agree)

I believe the cross and resurrection provide for my deepest need.

(strongly disagree)   1   2   3   4   5   (strongly agree)

I have seen God provide for things I have asked of him.

(strongly disagree)   1   2   3   4   5   (strongly agree)

I have seen God provide for my needs in ways I didn't ask.

(strongly disagree)   1   2   3   4   5   (strongly agree)

BIBLE INVESTIGATION

The following questions are designed to help you explore chapter 5 of Mark's Gospel. Take your time and write down your best response to each question.

1. For each of the three accounts in Mark 5, answer the following questions:

    a. What does each encounter in this passage tell us about Jesus' character?

        • Demon-possessed man

        • Suffering woman

        • Jairus and his daughter

    b. What does each encounter in this passage tell us about what it means to trust in Christ?

        • Demon-possessed man

- Suffering woman

- Jairus and his daughter

2. Review your responses to question 1. What common themes emerge in Mark 5?

GO DEEPER: Throughout Jesus' earthly ministry he encountered many forces that were beyond human control. Yet these forces obeyed Jesus because he had absolute authority over all things, including demons and death. In Mark 5 each person Jesus encountered experienced the effects of Jesus' power. He has the power and authority over all things including, and perhaps most importantly, the forgiveness of sin.

---

3. Read Mark 5:24, 30–32. If a large crowd "pressed" around him (v. 24), why did this one woman get Jesus' power and no one else?

4. In the four Gospels it isn't normal for Jesus to lose power when he performs a healing. Why would that happen in this case? What does that tell us about how Jesus heals us?

5. Read verses 21–25; 35–43. The healing of the woman came as an interruption to Jairus's miracle. What does the interruption teach you?

—◦◦✦◦◦—

Group Discussion

After a time of welcome and opening prayer, spend a few minutes reviewing your Pre-Group study together (observations, questions, insights), and then jump into this session's application questions and group exercise.

REVIEW

1. Open your Bible to Mark 5. Have one person summarize what happened in this chapter.

2. How did you respond to the first two statements in the Personal Reflection assessment, and why?

3. Share your answers to question 2 in the Bible Investigation section, exploring the common themes in Mark 5.

4. What other questions or insights do you have from your personal study?

APPLICATION

These questions are designed to help you take the core truths from the Introduction and Bible Investigation sections and introduce them into your story. Divide into smaller groups, if you wish.

> His power is unbounded, but so are his wisdom and his love.
> *Jesus the King,* p. 58

5. James 2:19 says, "You believe that there is one God. Good! Even the demons believe that—and shudder." How is your belief in Jesus supposed to be different from that of the demons here in Mark 5, who bowed down before Jesus in fear and trembling?

6. What was the point of Jesus singling out this woman in front of the crowd?

7. How is Jesus' response to the suffering woman an encouragement to those of us who are blind to many of our needs?

> We're not God, but we have such delusions of grandeur that our
> self-righteousness and arrogance sometimes have to be knocked
> out of our heart by God's delays.
>
> *Jesus the King*, p. 72

8. Describe a time when you experienced God's "delays."

9. Read Philippians 4:4–7. How can we have peace in Christ during circumstances, like Jairus's, that are prone to create anxiety and/or despair? *(The application of your answer here could be so powerful for you and those around you.)*

> If you go to Jesus, he may ask of you far more than you originally
> planned to give, but he can give you infinitely more than you dared
> ask or think.
>
> *Jesus the King*, p. 71

10. Where in your life are you waiting for Jesus to provide help?

How does Mark 5 change the way you believe in Jesus for that area of your life?

EXERCISE

Select one of the exercises below to engage the ideas in this session. Afterward, close in prayer.

OPTION 1: ACT IT OUT

Since this is week three together, and many people are visual and physical learners, it's time to have a little fun and break the ice. To help everyone in your group grasp the significance of the events, you are going to act out Mark 5 together. If possible, divide into three teams, with each team taking a different scene from the passage. There are plenty of characters, so a large group could involve almost everyone; a smaller group will need to "cast" the same actors in multiple parts. One person will be the narrator, with Mark 5 as the script. As the narrator reads the story, the actors perform. Enjoy!

OPTION 2: WRITE IT OUT

Divide into groups of at least two to three people. Assign each group one of the three scenes from Mark 5. Put yourself in the shoes of the person (Jairus, for example) and write a few sentences explaining your experience. Describe your life before meeting Jesus, what happened when you encountered Jesus, and how your life is different now. Come back together as a larger group and share your first-person accounts with one another.

—◦◦✦◦◦—

On Your Own

More deeply apply this session's truths by engaging in the Personal Challenge; then read ahead for next session.

PERSONAL CHALLENGE

Review your study guide responses over these first three sessions, which cover the first five chapters of Mark and the first six chapters of *Jesus the King*. Create a profile of Jesus based on what you have read thus far. The basic question you are answering is: "Up to this point, according to Mark, who is Jesus?"

READING ASSIGNMENT

Mark 6–7 and chapters 7–8 of *Jesus the King* by Timothy Keller

RIGHTLESS ASSERTIVENESS

Mark 7:14–37

—◦✦◦—

Pre-Group

Work through the following readings, Personal Reflection assessment, and Bible Investigation questions to prepare for the group gathering.

READING ASSIGNMENT

Mark 6–7 and chapters 7–8 of *Jesus the King* by Timothy Keller

INTRODUCTION

THE BIG IDEA

Only when you recognize that you have nothing to offer God, and yet he offers himself to you anyway, are you ready to come to him.

EMPTY TRADITIONS

One of the messages running through the Gospel of Mark, and throughout the rest of the Bible, is that God's grace — his undeserved mercy — is for all kinds of people. The Pharisees whom Jesus rebuked in 7:1–23 had an issue with this. They had created rituals and traditions over many generations to protect the exclusive audience they felt they had earned with God. The problem with these rituals was that they always shut people *out* of God's favor, sending the message that God's grace wasn't really for every sort of person. When Jesus' disciples started breaking some of the rules, the Pharisees criticized Jesus. The disciples were eating with unclean hands, which made them (according to tradition) ritually unclean before God. In response, Jesus exposed the emptiness of those traditions and declared that what was unclean under the tradition (certain foods) was clean in the eyes of God.

RIGHTLESS ASSERTIVENESS

Having discredited the man-made traditions, Jesus unveils new standards for who is worthy to approach God. Mark's very next scene (7:24–30) shows us a Syrophoenician woman who—according to Pharisaical practices—had no right to approach Jesus, and in desperation breaks through those traditional walls. By recounting how an unclean, Gentile woman at Jesus' feet is begging for help she doesn't deserve, Mark is tugging us to the edge of our seats. Just how far is Jesus going to go in breaking tradition? Jesus defers her initial request, which might have assuaged the Pharisees if it had ended there. But like any desperate mother, she is undeterred. She cares nothing for her pride, only for Jesus' power—a power so great and plentiful, she believes, that she only needs the crumbs. So when he insults her by calling her a dog, she accepts the label and asks for his power anyway.

Here is a woman exercising *rightless assertiveness*. She is basing her request solely on Jesus' goodness and not on her rights to it. Do you see her tears falling to the ground at his feet? Do you hear the hope in her voice as she pleads for mercy? As you read this scene, you are observing a model for how God wants us to approach him. Only when we are humbled by our utter dependence, desperate for Jesus' power, and confident in God's mercy, are we ready to approach God.

IT'S REALLY HIM!

Jesus grants this woman her request and sends the demon out of her daughter without even arising from the table, reminding us that he is in complete control of the spiritual realm. Mark then takes us to a scene where Jesus heals a deaf and mute man (7:31–37). Jesus takes an intimate approach in healing this man, and as he does, he shows his power over the physical realm as well. You can almost hear the disciples whispering again as they did in Mark 4:41: "Who is this? Even the wind and the waves obey him!" It is only beginning to dawn on them: *Is this who we think it is?*

An American soldier, due back home from his two-year tour of duty in the Middle East, was able to arrange to arrive a month early. With his wife's help, he managed to show up at his teenage daughter's dance recital, flowers and all, without her knowledge. When the daughter scanned the crowd after her performance and saw her dad, she immediately rushed to him, leapt into his arms, and, full of tears, cried, "Daddy, is it really you?"

The One you've waited on, the One you couldn't get to but longed to be with, has come. The One who makes demons flee, the deaf hear, and the mute speak abounds in mercy and is willing to give it to you. This is the good King, and he's really here.

PERSONAL REFLECTION

On a scale of 1–5 (1 = strongly disagree and 5 = strongly agree), select the number that best represents your response to each statement.

I feel desperate for God's mercy in my life.

(strongly disagree)   1   2   3   4   5   (strongly agree)

I try to abide by all of God's commands for my life as given in Scripture.

(strongly disagree)   1   2   3   4   5   (strongly agree)

I have a strong desire to know God more and more.

(strongly disagree)   1   2   3   4   5   (strongly agree)

I think I'm doing enough to earn at least some favor in God's eyes.

(strongly disagree)   1   2   3   4   5   (strongly agree)

I believe that God owes me good things.

(strongly disagree)   1   2   3   4   5   (strongly agree)

BIBLE INVESTIGATION

The following questions are designed to help you explore chapter 7 of Mark's Gospel. Take your time and write down your best response to each question.

1. Read Mark 7:14–23. What makes a person "unclean" or "defiled"?

2. What does Jesus mean by "defiled" and why is that so important to understanding the gospel message?

3. In your own words, explain what is being communicated through the dog metaphor in the exchange between Jesus and the woman.

4. What does the woman's reply to Jesus teach us about how we should approach God?

GO DEEPER: The way in which we approach God is very telling about how we view him and our relationship to him. The Syrophoenician woman approached God with a spirit of humility and absolute dependence. In Jesus she saw one overflowing with power and mercy. She readily accepted Jesus' label of her because her security was based in him, not in herself. To truly come to God will mean owning our true need as sinful and broken people, and at the same time leaning the hope of our lives on God's gracious and powerful nature to love us anyway.

---

5. What is surprising about the way Jesus heals the deaf and mute man?

6. Look up Isaiah 35:3–6 and use it to explain the bigger picture Mark wants us to see in Mark 7:31–37.

—⋘✠⋙—

Group Discussion

After a time of welcome and opening prayer, spend a few minutes reviewing your Pre-Group study together (observations, questions, insights), and then jump into this session's application questions and exercise.

REVIEW

1. Open your Bible to Mark 7. Have one person summarize what happened in Mark 7:14–37.

2. Based on your personal study, what do you think is the most challenging thing for you to understand from this passage? The most encouraging thing?

3. What is one thing God has been teaching or showing you about yourself during these first four weeks of the study?

APPLICATION

The following questions are designed to help you take the core truths from the Introduction and Bible Investigation sections and introduce them into your story.

4. Intentionally or not, almost every community of Christians sets up man-made "traditions" they expect people in good standing with God to follow. What could those traditions be in your local church or community?

> This is rightless assertiveness, something we know little about. She's not saying "Lord, give me what I deserve on the basis of my goodness." She's saying, "Give me what I *don't* deserve on the basis of *your* goodness — and I need it now."
>
> *Jesus the King*, p. 96

5. Why might it be offensive to claim that regardless of what we do, we are unworthy of God or have nothing to offer him?

6. How will the faith of the Gentile woman affect the way you approach God today?

7. What keeps you from being assertive in the way you approach God?

> Don't be too isolated to think you are beyond healing. Don't be too proud to accept what the gospel says about your unworthiness. Don't be too despondent to accept what the gospel says about how loved you are.
>
> *Jesus the King*, p. 102

8. Have you ever felt too broken or stained for God to love you? What does the gospel say about how loved you are?

EXERCISE

One of the purposes of this session is to help you realize your own helpless predicament when it comes to earning God's approval, which better enables you to understand the power of what Jesus did for you. This exercise (to be done individually, not as a group) is intended to help you internalize God's grace for you.

- **Step 1:** Write down several things that have happened to you, or things that you've said, done, or thought, that make you a flawed person. What in your life (past or present) makes you join with the apostle Paul, who once said, "I am the worst of sinners"? Do not spend more than two or three minutes on this list. And don't worry; you will not be asked to share your flaws and scars with anyone.

  -
  -
  -
  -
  -
  -
  -

- **Step 2:** Now beside or below this list write out the words of 2 Corinthians 5:17: "Therefore, if anyone is in Christ, the new creation has come: The old has gone, the new is here!"

- **Step 3:** Mark through the list you made so that you cannot see it anymore. Only the words of 2 Corinthians 5:17 should remain in front of you.

- **Step 4:** Spend a few minutes in silent prayer reflecting on God's powerful act of restoration he made available to you in Christ.

—◦◦✝◦◦—

On Your Own

More deeply apply this session's core truths by engaging in the Personal Challenge; then read ahead for next session.

PERSONAL CHALLENGE

Commit to spending at least ten minutes in prayer on five of the next seven days. If you'd like, you can pray right after completing your reading through the Gospel of Mark. Because this session has been about approaching God, make this an intentional theme of your prayers this week. Use this quote that was cited in the Application section to help guide you:

> Don't be too isolated to think you are beyond healing. Don't be too proud to accept what the gospel says about your unworthiness. Don't be too despondent to accept what the gospel says about how loved you are.
>
> *Jesus the King,* p. 102

In what areas of your life could you be isolated or despondent enough to think you are beyond healing, or to realize how loved you are? Ask God to give you his hope for healing and to enable you to see evidence of his love for you.

In what areas of your life could you be too proud to accept what the gospel says about your unworthiness? Ask God for his forgiveness and for the gift of humility.

Because seeing our thoughts often helps clarify them, write out these prayers as you go, either in a notebook or in the space provided on the next page. At the end of the week, read back through your prayers and evaluate them in light of what you've learned so far about how we are to approach God.

Prayer #1

Prayer #2

Prayer #3

Prayer #4

Prayer #5

READING ASSIGNMENT

Mark 8–9 and chapters 9–10 of *Jesus the King* by Timothy Keller

JESUS HAD TO DIE

Mark 8:27–31

---✦---

Pre-Group

Work through the following readings, Personal Reflection assessment, and Bible Investigation questions to prepare for the group gathering.

READING ASSIGNMENT

Mark 8–9 and chapters 9–10 of *Jesus the King* by Timothy Keller

INTRODUCTION

THE BIG IDEA

Jesus had to die to bring us life, and only when we deny ourselves and follow him can we share in that life.

THE QUESTION YOU MUST ANSWER

News demands evaluation. Whether it is a four-story advertisement in Times Square or a restaurant recommendation from a friend, we cannot help but assess a new message and respond to it. We are always interpreting messages through two filters: "Is it true?" and "Does it matter?" News about the latest turntables to play vinyl albums may be true, but it doesn't matter to most people.

When Jesus asked Peter, "Who do you say that I am?" he was asking Peter the question you and I must also answer. If it is true that Jesus is who he says he is, it matters supremely. Peter believed it was the truth—that Jesus was the Christ, the anointed King who would rule the world—which is why he devoted his life to following Jesus. The question for you is the same: *Who do you say Jesus is?* There is no more important question.

HE HAD TO DIE

Why would the Son of God have to die? This question confounds many Christians and non-Christians alike. It is hard to fathom why an all-powerful creator God would need to die to accomplish something. This line of thought leads to a perfectly reasonable question: Why wouldn't he just wave his hand, wipe away sin, and offer forgiveness like he created mountains and people? Peter's rebuke was packed with more freight, but his question was the same: Why go about it *like this*, Jesus?

Yet we know that the perfect God, the God we long for, cannot overlook evil. Evil results in a debt, which is why someone convicted of a crime is sentenced to pay the debt to society in some way. How can we ever repay an infinite debt to an infinitely holy God? When the people God loves commit the evil that requires the ultimate, absolutely just, but terrible payment—death (Romans 6:23), how can he respond? The cross is where the love and justice of God meet. Here he poured out the wrath that each of us owed for our rebellion against him. But in his love for us, he poured it on his Son instead. We deserved death, but in Christ we were given life.

WE MUST DIE AS WELL

Each time Jesus predicts his death in the Gospel of Mark he follows it with a statement about what it will look like to follow him with your life. Jesus looks at his disciples and the crowd around them and tells them that if they want to continue following him, they must deny themselves, pick up their cross, and follow him. Dietrich Bonhoeffer, a theologian and pastor who boldly resisted the Nazi regime, summarized this moment in his landmark book *The Cost of Discipleship* by saying "When Christ calls a man, he bids him come and die."

Jesus calls us to deny ourselves. That is, he calls us to surrender our own beliefs, priorities, and preferences that have created a false sense of reality around us. In this false life, we are in control and we turn ourselves into our own gods. This life, no matter how fulfilling it seems, is nothing more than a deeply rooted lie. The search for true life begins by denying the lie. At first this will feel like a form of death. In fact, the Bible's language for this type of surrender is to "die" to your current life. We are to "take up our cross" (Mark 8:34), a symbol in the first century of utter abandonment. We are to give up our right to self-determination. We agree to obey Jesus, whatever he tells us, and accept with courage and faith whatever he sends us. If we do not deny ourselves in this way, our personal agenda will always fight against the call of Jesus on our lives. To believe that the gospel message is true is to consider your former way of life dead. Jesus was clear: this is a costly belief. But the alternative is even costlier. We can follow Jesus, which is hard; or we can go our own way, which is even harder.

PERSONAL REFLECTION

On a scale of 1–5 (1 = strongly disagree and 5 = strongly agree), select the number that best represents your response to each of the following statements.

I regularly consider how my identity in Jesus should affect my daily activities.

    (strongly disagree)   1   2   3   4   5   (strongly agree)

I believe Jesus had to die.

    (strongly disagree)   1   2   3   4   5   (strongly agree)

I believe Jesus had to die *for my sins specifically*.

    (strongly disagree)   1   2   3   4   5   (strongly agree)

In Jesus Christ, I feel fully loved and forgiven by God today.

    (strongly disagree)   1   2   3   4   5   (strongly agree)

My friends and family can tell that I live knowing I am loved and forgiven by God.

    (strongly disagree)   1   2   3   4   5   (strongly agree)

BIBLE INVESTIGATION

The following questions are designed to help you explore chapter 8 of Mark's Gospel. Take your time and write down your best response to each question.

1. Read Psalm 2. "Christ" means anointed one. What characteristics of the "anointed one" do you see in this psalm?

2. According to Mark 8, why did Jesus tell the disciples to be quiet about him?

3. Read Daniel 7:13–14. How would you describe the "Son of Man" in this passage?

4. Mark 8:31 is where the entire book shifts in a new direction. Summarize in a sentence Mark's portrait of Jesus up to this point. How does what Jesus says in Mark 8:31 differ from the way Jesus has been previously presented?

5. In verse 31 the word *must* controls the sentence. What does this tell us about Jesus' purpose for coming to earth?

GO DEEPER: Mark gives us a detailed account of how Jesus revealed himself to the disciples as the expected Messiah sent from God. Yet what he came to do was vastly different than what the disciples anticipated. Jesus revealed he must suffer and die for the sins of his people, according to the Scriptures. This revelation, when finally understood, would redefine their expectations of Jesus and the way in which God would save his people. Jesus wasn't coming to lead an army; he was coming to die a desperate criminal's death that would give us life.

---

6. Why does Jesus rebuke Peter, and why so harshly?

7. In your own words, what is Jesus saying in verses 34–37?

—⊶✦⊷—

Group Discussion

After a time of welcome and opening prayer, spend a few minutes reviewing your Pre-Group study together (observations, questions, insights), and then jump into this session's application questions and group exercise.

REVIEW

1. Open your Bible to Mark 8. Have one person summarize what happens in Mark 8:27–37.

2. The Bible Investigation section focused on Mark 8:31. Why is that particular verse so important to understanding Mark's entire message?

3. What was your main takeaway from your personal study time?

APPLICATION

The following questions are designed to help you take the core truths from the Introduction and Bible Investigation sections and introduce them into your story.

> Jesus didn't say the Son of Man would suffer; he said that the Son of Man *must* suffer ... This is one of the most significant words in the story of the world, and it's a scary word.
>
> *Jesus the King*, pp. 105 – 106

4. Peter found the necessity of Jesus' death difficult. Why was this so difficult for him — and for us — to accept?

5. How is the interaction between Jesus and Peter a warning for us?

> Nobody can give anyone else the kind or amount of love they're starved for. In the end we're all alike, groping for true love and incapable of fully giving it. What we need is someone to love us who doesn't need us at all.
>
> *Jesus the King,* p. 107

6. Where do you personally look for true, satisfying love?

7. How should God's love for you affect the way you relate to your family and friends?

> Your real self will not come out as long as you are looking for it; it will only emerge when you're looking for him.
>
> *Jesus the King,* p. 116

8. What did it mean (or would it mean) for you to lose your life in order to follow Christ? Think of at least one tangible change.

9. In what part of your life do you still fight with God for control?

10. How does the gospel help you both submit to God and love him as you do it?

EXERCISE

In a group discussion it is easy for the rest of the group to hide behind affirming head nods to one person's answer. Sometimes, however, the stakes of the question are so high that it is worthwhile for everyone to have a chance to respond. Divide into pairs around the room, or in other rooms if available. Take turns, a couple minutes per person, processing the question, "Why did Jesus have to die?" Share which parts of the answer make sense to you and which don't. This may be the first time you and several others have ever verbally responded to this question, so be patient with one another. There are no points for eloquence or big words.

Then try to explain again, this time in terms that would make sense to someone who didn't grow up in the church and isn't a Christian. How can you do it without using terms like "sin" and "atonement" that Christians understand?

As you close the session time, pray for each other's opportunities for spiritual conversations in the coming week.

—◦⟨✛⟩◦—

On Your Own

More deeply apply this session's core truths by engaging in the Personal Challenge; then read ahead for next session.

PERSONAL CHALLENGE

In this week's Exercise you practiced explaining to a non-Christian friend why Jesus had to die. Write below the names of a couple of close non-Christian friends you would like to have a spiritual conversation with. Commit to pray for them, for your friendship with them, for their understanding and openness to God, and for your wisdom in sharing your view when the opportunity arises. Pray for each one specifically over the course of the next week, especially anticipating any times when you will see them. Commit to yourself that if the conversation does turn to spiritual things (and you are praying that it will), you will begin by asking questions and listening actively before sharing your own perspective. Come back to the next session ready to share your list of names and any encounters you had with people on your list.

READING ASSIGNMENT

Mark 10–12 and chapters 11–12 of *Jesus the King* by Timothy Keller

MAKING THE IMPOSSIBLE POSSIBLE

Mark 10:17–31; 12:28–34

—⟶⊹⟵—

Pre-Group

Work through the following readings, Personal Reflection assessment, and Bible Investigation questions to prepare for the group gathering.

READING ASSIGNMENT

Mark 10–12 and chapters 11–12 of *Jesus the King* by Timothy Keller

INTRODUCTION

THE BIG IDEA

Following Jesus will restructure how we approach every part of life, especially money and relationships.

NO OTHER MASTER

Many Christians are ready to give Jesus their allegiance, but he asks for more than that: he asks us to surrender what we treasure in our hearts—happiness, comfort, security, power, and love. For many, this is deeply uncomfortable. When Jesus pierces through the abstract and into the parts of our lives we give real value to, things get personal.

In chapter 10 Jesus talks with a young man who declares his allegiance to God through the ways he had followed the laws of God. But Jesus goes deeper than outward allegiance. He peers into the man's soul, finds his deepest love, and calls for him to give it away. The young man leaves saddened because this is a much bigger "ask" than he is ready for. Jesus looks out at a crowd after this rich young ruler sulks away and says, "It is easier for a camel to go through the eye of a needle than for a rich person to enter the kingdom of God" (v. 25 ESV). In other words—impossible.

It wasn't the money itself that kept this man from heaven; it was what the money meant. This man's riches were so critical to his security that even when he *wanted* to follow Jesus, he just couldn't part with that one precious thing—even though his riches had not brought him the heavenly security they promised. So his wealth had become a joyless master, one he would continue to serve even at the cost of his soul.

If there is any area of our lives where we refuse to let Jesus take hold, he'll press the issue—and we'll eventually release it to him and find joy, or grip it tighter and walk away from him unfulfilled.

This isn't a challenge only for the wealthy. In Mark 12:30 Jesus says the most important commandment is: "Love the Lord your God with all your heart and with all your soul and with all your mind and with all your strength." Rich and poor are in the same impossible predicament: anyone whose first love is not God himself can never enter God's kingdom. To enter the kingdom of heaven will mean to hand over everything to Jesus, especially the things to which we cling tightest. The beauty of this is, once we embrace him as our King, our hearts will begin to follow in affection for him. Then we can properly enjoy—as gracious gifts from God—those things that could never satisfy us as the source of our security.

We cannot make our way to God on our own, any more than we can buy ourselves absolute security and protection from pain. But he made a way to us, making the impossible possible.

PERSONAL REFLECTION

On a scale of 1–5 (1 = strongly disagree and 5 = strongly agree), select the number that best represents your response to each of the following statements.

I have something in my life right now I need more than I need Jesus.

(strongly disagree)   1   2   3   4   5   (strongly agree)

I aim to give financially in sacrificial ways that affect my lifestyle.

(strongly disagree)   1   2   3   4   5   (strongly agree)

I often get anxious about my financial situation.

(strongly disagree)   1   2   3   4   5   (strongly agree)

My confidence in my financial future comes more from my level of income and savings than from my understanding of how God will provide for everything I need.

(strongly disagree)   1   2   3   4   5   (strongly agree)

BIBLE INVESTIGATION

The following questions are designed to help you explore Mark 10:17–31 and 12:28–34. Take your time and write down your best response to each question.

Read Mark 10:17–31.

1. The gospel doesn't teach that we get our approval from God based on obeying the laws. So why is Jesus directing the rich young ruler toward the commandments in his first response?

Romans 7:7

2. Notice verse 21 where Mark pauses to tell us Jesus looked at this man and "loved him." How is Jesus' next response to the young man an act of love?

3. What does Jesus teach about wealth, riches, and the Christian faith in verses 17–31?

GO DEEPER: Throughout the Gospel of Mark we see Jesus respond to people in different ways to show them their need for him. Some people approached him in desperation, and to them he was the answer they'd been longing for. Others approached him with hesitation, still clinging to something other than Christ to save them. To these, Jesus revealed the futility of hope placed in anything other than him. Similarly, when Jesus points out to the rich young ruler that he needs to give all his things away, he is asking him to demote whatever holds top priority in his heart. The only way this man can truly find happiness in God is to see that his greatest need for security is met in Jesus, not money.

4. In light of Jesus' statement in verse 27, explain how it is impossible for anyone to enter the kingdom of heaven and at the same time *possible for anyone* to enter the kingdom of heaven.

Read Mark 12:28–34.

5. Read Deuteronomy 6:4–5 and Leviticus 19:18. These were two significant statements for Israel, though they aren't anywhere near each other in the Old Testament. Why does Jesus emphasize them together here in Mark?

6. How does this encounter with the teacher of the law reinforce Jesus' encounter with the rich young ruler?

—◦◦✦◦◦—

Group Discussion

After a time of welcome and opening prayer, spend a few minutes reviewing your Pre-Group study together (observations, questions, insights), and then jump into this session's application questions and group exercise.

REVIEW

1. Open your Bible to Mark 10. Have one person summarize what happened in Mark 10:17–31.

2. What point stuck out to you the most from your personal study?

3. Share your responses to question 4. Are there any other questions from the Bible Investigation that you would like to discuss further?

APPLICATION

The following questions are designed to help you take the core truths from the Introduction and Bible Investigation sections and introduce them into your story.

> The center of Christianity is always migrating away from power and wealth.
>
> *Jesus the King*, p. 136

4. What is it about the gospel that puts it at odds with power and wealth?

> Jesus was saying that there is something radically wrong with *all* of us — but money has particular power to blind us to it. In fact, it has so much power to deceive us of our true spiritual state that we need a gracious, miraculous intervention from God to see it.
>
> *Jesus the King*, p. 140

5. What is the spiritual problem money blinds us to?

6. What are the things in your life that trigger anxiety?

7. How can you pursue a successful career and not succumb to the trap wealth creates?

> If you understand that Jesus is the true Rich Young Ruler, it is going to change your attitude to money. For example, you won't be trying to figure out how much you *have* to give away; you'll try to figure out how much you *can* give away.
>
> *Jesus the King*, p. 149

8. What are some ways the gospel has changed—or could change—your attitude toward money?

9. Sometimes the greatest commandment seems the hardest and most debilitating to many Christians. How can we obey this impossible command to "love God" in a way that is life-giving instead of life-draining?

EXERCISE

The church of the New Testament was marked by their generosity toward one another and toward the communities they lived in. Still today, one of the most contagious things about a group of Christians is their generosity. In light of this session's emphasis on loving Christ over money, brainstorm a specific need or opportunity your group could collectively provide for. Maybe it is a friend in need or a local organization (school, charity, etc.) that could use some help. The goal is to practice joy-infected generosity with someone outside of your group. Think of this as a practice run at what life would look like if your affections were set primarily on the God of the gospel instead of anything else. To honor the short-term nature of this study, make this exercise a one-time thing. You may decide later to make it an ongoing act of generosity, but that's up to the group. To help get the conversation going:

- Who (or what organization) do you know that is in a specific place of need right now?

- If we dream big enough, what could we do as a group to generously meet that need?

- What dreams of renewal do you have for your community that you would love to work and contribute toward?

For example: One group who did this exercise had a group member whose rock-climbing partner injured himself and was without insurance. The group footed the entire medical bill (no small matter), and the man was overwhelmed. When he visited the group weeks later and asked them why they did what they did, they explained their generosity in terms of the gospel. Soon after, he decided to become a Christian. He attributed his conversion to how God used a group of people to show him radical generosity in a way he simply couldn't ignore or understand.

As you conclude your time together, pray that people will see the love of Christ through whatever expression of generosity your group commits to.

—◦◦✝◦◦—

On Your Own

More deeply apply this session's core truths by engaging in the Personal Challenge; then read ahead for next session.

PERSONAL CHALLENGE

In Matthew 6:21 Jesus says, "Where your treasure is, there your heart will be also." We spend money on what we care about. This challenge is designed to help you take a next step toward realigning your affections to Christ. Take a few minutes alone to write down your personal budget. If you've never done this before, simply write down what you spend money on and how much you spend on each category. This doesn't need to be precise, just "ballpark" enough to help you get a fair picture of your spending habits.

Once you are done, take a moment to consider how this budget reflects what you value. (Few people feel like they are living in excessive luxury, so don't be surprised if you can make a good case for everything in your budget. Indeed, there are likely many good things on your budget related to your home, your family, your future, etc.) Obviously, a budget isn't a perfect indicator of everything you value, but what does yours say are your top three priorities? List them here.

Priority #1

Priority #2

Priority #3

If you desire Christ to be the top priority in your life, how might you adjust your budget to reflect that?

READING ASSIGNMENT

Mark 13–14 and chapters 13–14 of *Jesus the King* by Timothy Keller

COMMUNION AND COMMUNITY

Mark 14:12–25

—◦◦✦◦◦—

Pre-Group

Work through the following readings, Personal Reflection assessment, and Bible Investigation questions to prepare for the group gathering.

READING ASSIGNMENT

Mark 13–14 and chapters 13–14 of *Jesus the King* by Timothy Keller

INTRODUCTION

THE BIG IDEA

Jesus' sacrifice provides our souls with food and turns our broken relationships into a beautiful family.

THE COVERING OF COMMUNION

J. K. Rowling's heralded *Harry Potter* series is the story of a talented young wizard who was orphaned as a baby. During his first year at wizard school, Harry's headmaster and mentor Albus Dumbledore tells him that Harry's parents died protecting him from an attack by the powerful and wicked Voldemort. Harry's only connection to that tragic night is a peculiarly shaped scar on his forehead. In describing the sacrifice Harry's mother made for him, Dumbledore explains:

> "Your mother died to save you. If there is one thing Voldemort cannot understand, it is love. He didn't realize that love as powerful as your mother's for you leaves its own mark. Not a scar, no visible sign … [T]o have been loved so deeply, even though the person who loved us is gone, will give us some protection forever."

Communion is the church's mark, or *sign*, that points us back to the moment Jesus died to save us. In Mark 14:22–23 Jesus presides over a Passover meal where he calls the bread his body and the wine his blood. When we eat the bread and drink from the cup we are transported back to the cross where his body was crucified and his blood poured out in death.

Death, you see, was to be *our* penalty for *our* rebellion against God. But Jesus loved us so deeply that he took *our* death and made it *his*. His payment covered our debt. He stepped in front of the judgment coming for us and took it himself. When Jesus sits down with his disciples in Mark 14, this is the simple and profound message behind the meal: we are saved by his death. And the meal provides us with the opportunity to live in awareness of his life-giving death. No wonder he tells the church to share the feast so often.

THE TRUE FEAST AND TRUE FAMILY

In a fractious and divisive world where every generation yearns for the cohesion and power of community, nothing else is like communion. It celebrates the most important moment in history and provides us with an unparalleled opportunity to experience the oneness we are given in the death of Christ.

Every time a local church practices communion together, they harmonize each of their personal stories together into a unified celebration. Communion is like an orchestra composed of dozens of different instruments, all equally focused on a single piece of music, made all the more beautiful by the intricate diversity of sounds. Each believer who takes the bread and the cup has a unique story of salvation in Christ. But it is *one* story, and at the communion meal, the story that binds each person's story together rises to the top. Though one came from poverty and another from wealth, one from brokenness and addiction and another from self-righteous religiosity, one is black and another is white, all hold the same bread and the same cup. Their stories unite like various instruments in one harmonious moment, proclaiming together their belief that the death of Jesus makes them a new family. Their differences are no match for their unity in the blood of Christ.

Here is the true feast our hungry hearts have longed for. Here, in this act of remembering Jesus' sacrifice, is the true family our broken and divisive world desires.

Christ did not merely save us *from* something; he saved us *to* something—to a community. To a family that feasts together on the hope given to us in Jesus, so that we can share that hope with the world. Are you a part of that family?

PERSONAL REFLECTION

On a scale of 1–5 (with 1 = strongly disagree and 5 = strongly agree), select the number that best represents your response to each of the following statements.

I believe the death of Christ covers the debt I owe because of my sin.

(strongly disagree)　1　2　3　4　5　(strongly agree)

I could explain the meaning of Passover and communion (and the difference between them) to a friend if asked.

(strongly disagree)　1　2　3　4　5　(strongly agree)

I feel that my local church is more than a place I attend; it is a family that I am a part of.

(strongly disagree)　1　2　3　4　5　(strongly agree)

I take communion with my local church family regularly.

(strongly disagree)　1　2　3　4　5　(strongly agree)

I need to be closer to people in my church family than I am right now.

(strongly disagree)　1　2　3　4　5　(strongly agree)

BIBLE INVESTIGATION

The following questions are designed to help you explore Mark 14:12–25. Take your time and write down your best response to each question.

1. The details provided in verses 12–16 appear peripheral to the story. Why do you think Mark includes this seemingly inconsequential part of the story for his readers?

2. To understand Mark 14:12–25 we must understand the Passover meal Jesus is sharing with his disciples. Read Exodus 12:1–14 to learn the history of the very first Passover meal. List the specific actions God told each Israelite family to take in these verses.

3. In your own words, how would you describe the scene depicted in this passage from Exodus 12?

4. Now reread Mark 14:12–25 and compare it to what you just read in Exodus 12. What parallels do you see in these two scenes?

5. Make a list of everything we learn specifically about the meaning of Christ's death from this teaching that he is our Passover lamb.

6. Now summarize in one sentence the meaning of Christ as the Passover lamb.

GO DEEPER: The shedding of a lamb's blood caused the Spirit of God to "pass over" and spare God's people before their exodus, or escape, from judgment in Egypt. The Passover was a foreshadowing of the deliverance, or salvation, Jesus would bring to his people. Jesus was the sacrificial lamb who shed his own blood, bringing salvation and forgiveness to all those who would believe in him. When he took the place of the Passover lamb he was declaring his blood to be the means of salvation for all who are willing to stake their hopes on it.

—◦◦✦◦◦—

Group Discussion

After a time of welcome and opening prayer, spend a few minutes reviewing your Pre-Group study together (observations, questions, insights), and then jump into this session's application questions and group exercise.

REVIEW

1. Open your Bible to Mark 14. Have one person summarize what happened in Mark 14:12–25.

2. How did your personal study help you understand the purpose and practice of communion?

3. What other key insights did you gain from studying the passage or from reading chapters 13–14 of *Jesus the King*?

APPLICATION

The following questions are designed to help you take the core truths from the Introduction and Bible Investigation sections and introduce them into your story.

> With the simple words "This is my body . . . this is my blood," Jesus is saying that all the earlier deliverances, the earlier sacrifices, the lambs at Passover, were pointing to himself.
>
> *Jesus the King,* p. 182

4. The Israelites needed a sacrificial lamb to spare themselves from the angel of death who was coming to judge Egypt. But our situation is different. Why do we need a "sacrificial lamb," and why Jesus?

5. Jesus offers the bread to the disciples and tells them they must *take* it. What are some things that need to happen in your heart and mind so that you can sincerely take what Jesus is offering?

> All love, all real, life-changing love, is substitutionary sacrifice.
>
> *Jesus the King,* p. 183

6. Describe a time when you received truly substitutionary, sacrificial love.

7. Think about the people and situations in your life. What situations require you to give real substitutionary, sacrificial love? Be specific.

> When you take the Lord's Supper, you are doing it with brothers and sisters, with family. This bond is so life-transforming that it creates a basis for unity as strong as if people had been raised together.
>
> *Jesus the King,* p. 187

8. When you think of "family," is that a positive or negative thing for you? *(Because this could really open up a rabbit trail better suited for another group time, try to explain your answer in no more than a sentence or two.)*

9. What is one practical step this group could take to become more like family members to one another?

10. What is one practical step you could take to become more like a family member in your local church?

EXERCISE

A lighthearted saying around many churches is, "A group that eats together, stays together." That's not always true, but it certainly sounds good, and groups that enjoy one another do fare better. For this week's group exercise, you are going to plan a family meal together. All the meal decisions are going to be made right here, right now. The theme of the meal? *Family time.* Whatever that means for your group is up to you. Before you leave this gathering, be sure to make firm plans. If you need help, here are four questions to answer to plan a family dinner:

1. What night?

Ideally the meal will happen on an alternate night during the week so that you do not feel a time crunch to work through both the study and dinner. If schedules are too difficult to manage, you can plan on eating together prior to the next session. But reserve at least one hour for eating together. This should not be rushed!

2. What to eat?

Will you bring covered dishes from each family's favorite meals? Will you cook together? Is there a chef in the group? A grill master? Is there a pizza carry-out place nearby? It's up to you, but decide the general meal plans *now*.

3. Who is bringing the "other stuff"?

You know, plates and cups and drinks. Help the host out a bit. Speaking of which . . .

4. Where?

Assuming you have been meeting in a home, perhaps someone else in the group would like to take a turn at hosting a gathering. This is a low-risk way to do that without asking the weekly host to double up responsibilities.

Dinner Topic: One way to make the most of your dinner would be to take some time to share your family stories together. You know, that longer story you wanted to share in question 8 but didn't have time for.

—◦✦◦—

On Your Own

More deeply apply this session's core truths by engaging in the Personal Challenge; then read ahead for next session.

PERSONAL CHALLENGE

In 1 Corinthians 11:17 – 33 Paul gives instructions to the church about taking communion, part of which you looked at in this session. In verses 27 – 32 Paul calls believers to "examine themselves" lest they eat the bread and drink the cup in an unworthy manner. To examine yourself most likely means to assess your spiritual health, much like a physician would assess your physical health in a routine checkup. In preparation for the next time your local church takes communion together, spend some time examining your own life as a Christian. Here are a few questions to get you started:

What unconfessed sin do you need to repent of? Confess it to God and repent, asking him to continue to turn your affections toward him and away from sin.

Who are you in conflict with? Confess these conflicts to God and then seek reconciliation.

In which areas of your life are you resisting God's guidance or delaying obedience? Confess your rebellious attitude and ask God to continue to shepherd you toward the path of wisdom. Close by thanking God for providing healing and forgiveness for these things you have identified in your life.

READING ASSIGNMENT

Mark 14 – 15 and chapters 15 – 17 of *Jesus the King* by Timothy Keller

THE CRUCIFIED KING

Mark 14:53–65; 15:1–34

—◦❦◦—

Pre-Group

Work through the following readings, Personal Reflection assessment, and Bible Investigation questions to prepare for the group gathering.

READING ASSIGNMENT

Mark 14–15 and chapters 15–17 of *Jesus the King* by Timothy Keller

INTRODUCTION

THE BIG IDEA

The King willingly died for his rebel people.

DEATH TO THE KING

Throughout history, when a monarch is dethroned, it is always against his will and out of his control. Before Charles I of England was beheaded in 1649—by his own countrymen—he waged a civil war trying to regain control and retain his crown. Kings do not *willingly* die at the hands of their own people. Certainly not kings who also ascribe divinity to themselves. Yet in chapters 14 and 15, Mark shows us "The King of the Jews" as he willingly allows himself to be beaten, mocked, and killed by his own people.

On the face of it, the crucifixion story seems like a shocking oxymoron. God could never stoop to the humiliation of trial, torture, and execution by his creatures. But Mark wants to be clear to his readers that the man going to the cross, the man going to his death, is indeed God. Jesus owns his divine kingship claim when questioned by the ruling council and again by Pilate. In Jesus, God is willingly subjecting himself to death on a cross for his rebellious people — for you and me.

INTO THE DARKNESS FOR US

The shroud of supernatural darkness punctuating that ominous day creates a multisensory message to the reader that Jesus is being condemned not just by man but by God. Why would he suffer this brutality? The answer gets at the core of the Christian message: the pain of his death and (much worse) the horror of the Father's silence were outweighed by his love for us. As Luke records, Jesus looks down at his killers and uses his dying breath to plead for forgiveness.

What is your reaction to the scene as Mark depicts it? Are you upset at the angry mob conspiring to kill Jesus? Are you, like many of his admirers, confused or frustrated by Jesus' submission to this torture? Are you disappointed in Peter and the disciples for abandoning him in his greatest time of need? Are you frustrated with Pilate for handing him over? Are you horrified by the ones who drove the nails into his hands and feet? Are you disgusted by the mockers who divided his garments?

What if you read yourself into the place of each of those characters? In our stubborn selfishness, we do what each of the characters in this scene does. Our sin comes from our desire to control our lives, so though Jesus claims kingship over us, we rebel against him, we reject him, deny him, and crucify him. We are the mob.

Yet in the great and beautiful paradox of substitutionary sacrifice, our mob allegiance is good news for us. Christ went to the cross *for the sake of that mob*, so that you and I could go past the curtain that once stood between us and God. The curtain was torn from the top down because God was making a way for us to come back home to him. Though you have been a part of the mob, perhaps you can now confess with the centurion, "Surely this man was the Son of God!"

PERSONAL REFLECTION

On a scale of 1–5 (1 = strongly disagree and 5 = strongly agree), select the number that best represents your response to each of the following statements.

I can relate to the motivations of the angry mob that killed Jesus.

(strongly disagree)   1   2   3   4   5   (strongly agree)

There are areas of my life where I deny or neglect my allegiance to Jesus.

(strongly disagree)   1   2   3   4   5   (strongly agree)

I sometimes feel like I am in darkness I can't escape.

(strongly disagree)   1   2   3   4   5   (strongly agree)

I believe I should submit to Jesus, because he is the King.

(strongly disagree)   1   2   3   4   5   (strongly agree)

I want to submit to Jesus even if that gets difficult.

(strongly disagree)   1   2   3   4   5   (strongly agree)

BIBLE INVESTIGATION

The following questions are designed to help you explore Mark 14:53–65; 15:1–34. Take your time and write down your best response to each question.

1. Look at the accusation made against Jesus in Mark 14:58. Though it is a false accusation—Jesus never said he would destroy the temple—how is it in some part pointing to the truth of what Jesus came to do?

2. Compare the questions of the high priest (14:61) and of Pilate (15:2) and how Jesus responds to both. What does Mark want his readers to take away from these interrogations?

3. Read Mark 15:17–20, 29–32. Why is Jesus mocked, and why might Mark want his readers to experience this?

4. Some have called Mark 15:34 "the most important and terrible question ever asked." What does the question tell us about what Jesus is doing? What does it tell us about what the Father is doing? What is the answer to Jesus' question?

GO DEEPER: The cross is a gruesome depiction of the spiritual reality of our sin. We don't often think about our sin having such physically horrifying consequences. Yet when God turned away from Jesus as he hung on the cross, it was justice served on our sin. Because of it, God forsook Jesus on the cross so that you and I would never be forsaken by him. With our debt paid, we are free to be reconciled to the Father. This is the salvation and acceptance each of us is longing for.

---

5. Read Hebrews 10:19–20. What is the meaning of the tearing of the temple curtain in Mark 15:38?

6. Read Hebrews 10:21–25. How should Christians respond to the tearing of the temple curtain?

7. What response from his readers do you think Mark is looking for by including the confession of the centurion in Mark 15:39?

—◦◦◦✝◦◦◦—

Group Discussion

After a time of welcome and opening prayer, spend a few minutes reviewing your Pre-group study together (observations, questions, insights), and then jump into this session's application questions and group exercise.

REVIEW

1. Open your Bible to Mark 14–15. Have one person summarize what happened in Mark 14:53–15:34.

2. Discuss your responses to question 4 from the Bible Investigation section.

3. What other observations or insights did you find to be helpful from your personal study?

APPLICATION

The following questions are designed to help you take the core truths from the Introduction and Bible Investigation sections and introduce them into your story.

> He is the judge over the entire world, being judged by the world. He should be in the judgment seat, and we should be in the dock, in chains. Everything is turned upside down.
>
> *Jesus the King,* p. 214

4. What do the descriptions of the mocking, spitting, and beating tell us about human nature?

5. While you and I cannot literally spit in Jesus' face, we can still mock and reject him. In what ways are you prone to reject Jesus as God?

> It is noteworthy that Mark gives us very few of the gory details. He aims the spotlight away from the physical horrors of Jesus' ordeal in order to focus it on the deeper meaning behind the events.
>
> *Jesus the King*, p. 217

6. The arrest, trial, and death of Jesus are the scenes that build to the climax of his resurrection. In one or two sentences, summarize the meaning of the arrest, trial, and death of Jesus.

7. How can Jesus' cry to God be a help to you when you feel alone and forsaken (even by God)?

> When you are in spiritual darkness, although you may feel your life is headed in the right direction, you are actually profoundly disoriented.
>
> *Jesus the King*, p. 222

8. Describe a time when you've experienced spiritual darkness in your own life.

9. How does the gospel provide the "way out" of spiritual darkness?

EXERCISE

The session 1 Personal Challenge was to write your spiritual story in 500 words or less. Now that you've become better acquainted with the other members of your group, it's time to share that story. Divide into groups of three, turn back to the "My Spiritual Story" page, and take turns sharing. Remember, these are *short* stories that should take no more than five minutes to tell. While telling your story, answer this question: *What have you learned/experienced in this small group that adds to your spiritual story?*

Once you are finished, come back together and recommend one or two stories that can be retold to the entire group. Have your "nominees" share their stories, and then close out the session in prayer.

—◦◦✦◦◦—

On Your Own

More deeply apply this session's core truths by engaging in the Personal Challenge; then read ahead for next session.

PERSONAL CHALLENGE

Sometimes the idea of "following Jesus" can seem so daunting and abstract that we never really get started. We *want* to grow but don't know how to get beyond where we are right now. This week's challenge is to identify your "next step" in following Jesus. The entire *Jesus the King* study has built on the premise that you are created to center your entire life on God—and his gospel is both the reason and the means by which you do that. A life centered on God is one motivated by his love for you and marked by steps of gospel obedience. So, what is *your* next step? Choose from the following list or create your own step.

- I will surrender my need to control some area of my life over to Jesus as my God and King. In the next 30 days, I will commit to obey God in this area (e.g., my marriage), whatever that means.

- To follow God, I need to know him better, so I'm going to use a Bible reading plan to develop a consistent daily time in the Bible.

- I will live and forgive others as I have been fully forgiven by my King. I will start by forgiving _____ and confessing my unforgiveness to God.

- Because money has such potential power over me, I'm going to give away 50 percent of what I would otherwise spend on _____ in the next month.

- Because I need to be an active part of a Christian community, I commit to getting involved in a local church/small group.

- Other:

Note: The danger of a challenge like this is that you can begin to believe you can manufacture spiritual vitality, which in the Christian faith is simply not true. That said, obedience to Christ does create a heart and mind tuned into what God is doing in and through you. Because we are prone to drift away from Christ, obedience to him requires intentionality.

READING ASSIGNMENT

Mark 15–16 and chapters 18 and "After" of *Jesus the King* by Timothy Keller

—⁕—

THE DEATH OF DEATH

Mark 15:40–16:8

—◦◦✦◦◦—

Pre-Group

Work through the following readings, Personal Reflection assessment, and Bible Investigation questions to prepare for the group gathering.

READING ASSIGNMENT

Mark 15–16 and chapters 18 and "After" of *Jesus the King* by Timothy Keller

INTRODUCTION

THE BIG IDEA

The resurrection of Jesus changes everything for us now.

IT REALLY HAPPENED

Much as he has in the rest of the story, Mark takes a reporter's approach to describing this last and most unbelievable scene: the resurrection. He draws attention to the overwhelming evidence of the event so that his readers—assured that it happened—are left to grapple with how to respond to it. The list of witnesses to the death, the details of the burial, and the shocking discovery of the empty tomb are Mark's way of giving eyewitness accounts to an event that—despite Jesus' repeated hints and promises—still caught everyone by surprise.

And even when presented with the evidence, many people still refused to accept that this man, brutally and publicly executed, had somehow walked out of his tomb. The same is true today. Some say Jesus wasn't *actually* dead and that his "resurrection" was merely resuscitation. Others say that he did die and the entire resurrection account is a hoax perpetuated to bolster the Christian faith. Every skeptical theory has one underlying starting point: the resurrection couldn't have happened. And we should expect a high level of scrutiny regarding the resurrection. Because if it *did* happen—if Jesus really did make it out of the grave alive—everything changes.

Why? The death of Jesus, as we've seen, is of critical importance. It proves our sin was so serious that Jesus had to die for us; and that he loved us so much he was willing to do so. But if it had ended there, we might have been moved, but we wouldn't have had any true hope for ourselves, for our future, or for our world.

THE RESURRECTION CHANGES EVERYTHING

I (Spence) will never forget praying over an eighteen-year-old friend in the final days of his fight with cancer. We didn't expect to see him at worship that morning, but he was determined to come. It was to be his last service with his church family before he died. When his parents wheeled him up, he asked us to pray that the hope of the resurrection of Jesus would triumph in his heart over the fear of impending death. Because Jesus had gotten out of the grave, he was able to believe with the apostle Paul that "death has no sting." This wasn't spiritual rhetoric for him; it was a battle cry in the face of a fierce enemy. The imminence of death was being overshadowed by the certainty of the glory awaiting him in the presence of Jesus.

The power of the resurrection lies in its freedom. While most of us in the Western world live our daily lives immune to major tragedy, we all share an unspoken yet constant insecurity that everything could, at some point, fall apart. We know enough to know nothing is certain, so we toil to build levees to buttress some unknown impending flood that could ruin our lives. Yet the levees never seem secure enough. Death always looms.

The resurrection of Jesus is freedom from the insatiable need to build greater levees of security. The resurrection secures victory over any and all pain that awaits us. It promises that the darkness of this world will not have the final say. So instead of enslaving ourselves to an illusion of security, we can live as free people, secured by the certain hope that glory, not tragedy, is on the other side of the horizon.

PERSONAL REFLECTION

On a scale of 1–5 (1 = strongly disagree and 5 = strongly agree), select the number that best represents your response to each of the following statements.

I believe Jesus died and then rose again. *(You cannot somewhat agree with this one. Agree or disagree?)*

        (strongly disagree)   1   2   4   5   (strongly agree)

I find myself worrying less about my circumstances because of the resurrection.

        (strongly disagree)   1   2   3   4   5   (strongly agree)

I am a little envious of the way I see other Christians live with more hope than I do.

        (strongly disagree)   1   2   3   4   5   (strongly agree)

There are some real things I'm afraid of right now.

        (strongly disagree)   1   2   3   4   5   (strongly agree)

I trust that one day God will make all of the mess of this world into something brand new.

        (strongly disagree)   1   2   3   4   5   (strongly agree)

BIBLE INVESTIGATION

The following questions are designed to help you explore Mark 15:42–47; 16:1–8. Take your time and write down your best response to each question.

1. Read Mark 15:42–47. List the evidence Mark gives to certify that Jesus is dead.

2. What should we take away from the fact that the witnesses and people showing faithfulness to Jesus are Joseph, a Pharisee (15:40–47); women (16:1–8); and a Roman centurion (15:39, 44)?

3. Why is it important that in such a short retelling, Mark places a clear emphasis on the historicity of the death and resurrection of Jesus?

GO DEEPER: The resurrection of Jesus is one of the most scrutinized events in human history. Mark wants to make sure his readers believe the resurrection actually happened. Because if it really happened, then Jesus really is God and we can be fully and permanently accepted by him; and there really is hope for us in and beyond this broken world. It means Mark's readers were, and still are, free from the anxieties of this world because their hope is secured in their eternal standing with God.

4. Jesus' appearance seemed to surprise Mary, Mary, and Salome. It also surprised the rest of the disciples when he appeared to them, as told in the other Gospel accounts. If Jesus told them he would rise again, why were they so surprised?

5. Read Luke 24:36–47. Luke provides even more details of Jesus' post-resurrection appearances. What evidence here attests to the veracity of the resurrection?

6. In one sentence, explain what the resurrection means for you. What does and doesn't make sense to you about the resurrection?

—⟨❦⟩—

Group Discussion

After a time of welcome and opening prayer, spend a few minutes reviewing your Pre-Group study together (observations, questions, insights), and then jump into this session's application questions and group exercise.

REVIEW

1. Open your Bible to Mark 15–16. Have one person summarize what happened in Mark 15:40–16:8.

2. What did you learn about the resurrection from your personal study?

3. What questions remain unanswered for you relating to Mark's account of the death and resurrection of Jesus?

APPLICATION

The following questions are designed to help you take the core truths from the Introduction and the Bible Investigation sections and introduce them into your story.

> The resurrection was as inconceivable for the first disciples, as impossible for them to believe, as it is for many of us today.
>
> *Jesus the King*, p. 236

4. Why are people skeptical about the historicity of the resurrection of Jesus?

5. Is it difficult for *you* to believe Jesus rose from the dead? Why or why not?

> The truth of the resurrection is of supreme and eternal importance. It is the hinge upon which the story of the world pivots.
>
> *Jesus the King*, p. 242

6. How does Jesus' resurrection give you hope? Be specific.

7. How can the resurrection offer hope to a single community? To a broken world?

> So live in the light of the resurrection and renewal of this world, and of yourself, in a glorious, never-ending, joyful dance of grace.
> *Jesus the King*, p. 246

8. Reflect on your time in this study. How would you summarize the message of Mark's Gospel in a single thought?

9. How has your time in this group study changed your belief about yourself and about God?

EXERCISE

Acknowledging the end of a shared experience is important to help you move forward with what you've learned. This group exercise is designed to send you out, just as Jesus sent out his disciples as he left them—to the far corners of the earth in the power of his Holy Spirit and with the great news of the gospel he'd taught them.

Jesus sends *you* with the same power and news—to your friends, your family, your various networks, your vocation, and maybe even to the ends of the world. As a group, spend time in prayer, thanking God for the things he has taught you. Pray for one another to go out from here in the joyful grace of God that you've discussed and experienced together. Lastly, pray for the chance to take this great and true story to others who haven't heard it yet. Have one person finish the prayer time by reading Psalm 67 aloud in benediction over the group:

> [1]May God be gracious to us and bless us and make his face shine on us—[2]so that your ways may be known on earth, your salvation among all nations. [3]May the peoples praise you, God; may all the peoples praise you. [4]May the nations be glad and sing for joy, for you rule the peoples with equity and guide the nations of the earth. [5]May the peoples praise you, God; may all the peoples praise you. [6]The land yields its harvest; God, our God, blesses us. [7]May God bless us still, so that all the ends of the earth will fear him.

—◦◦✝◦◦—

On Your Own

More deeply apply this session's core truths by engaging in the Personal Challenge.

PERSONAL CHALLENGE

As you conclude this small group experience, the challenge going forward is to dwell on the beautiful mystery of the gospel every day. Jesus said to simply "abide in him" and you will bear much fruit. So abide, or make your home in, your King Jesus Christ. The more you get to know him, the more overwhelmed you will be by the heights of his holiness, the depths of your sin, and the riches of his grace that bridge the two. Use what you prepared from the session 7 Personal Challenge to take that next step toward Jesus and his unyielding love for you.

Conversations on Faith and Life

In his book *The Reason for God*, Timothy Keller established himself as a modern-day C. S. Lewis who brings together faith and intellect, theology and popular culture, modern-day objections and historic Christian beliefs.

Now fans of the *New York Times* bestseller can use this same rich content in a six-session video study, ideal for small groups, individuals, or any believer who is engaging with friends who don't share his or her beliefs.

While *The Reason for God* DVD captures a live and unscripted conversation between Timothy Keller and six panelists discussing their objections to Christianity, the Discussion Guide helps small groups and individuals dig deeper into the objections of the Christian faith and to learn about both sides of the issues.

Discussion Guide, 978-0-310-33047-9
DVD, 978-0-310-33046-2
Discussion Guide and DVD, 978-0-310-61897-3

1. Isn't the Bible a Myth? Hasn't Science Disproved Christianity?

2. How Can You Say There Is Only One Way to God? What About Other Religions?

3. What Gives You the Right to Tell Me How to Live My Life? Why Are There So Many Rules?

4. Why Does God Allow Suffering? Why Is There So Much Evil in the World?

5. Why Is the Church Responsible for So Much Injustice? Why Are Christians Such Hypocrites?

6. How Can God Be Full of Love and Wrath at the Same Time? How Can God Send Good People to Hell?

AVAILABLE ONLINE OR AT YOUR FAVORITE BOOKSTORE!

ZONDERVAN

www.redeemercitytocity.com
www.gospelinlife.com

REDEEMER **CITY to CITY**

gospel in life is an intensive eight-session course on the gospel and how it is lived out in all of life—first in your heart, then in your community, and then out into the world.

Session 1 opens the course with the theme of the city: your home now, the world that is. Session 8 closes the course with the theme of the eternal city: your heavenly home, the world that is to come. In between, you will look at how the gospel changes your heart (sessions 2 and 3), changes your community (sessions 4 and 5), and changes how you live in the world (sessions 6 and 7).

1 **City** The World That Is

2 **Heart** Three Ways To Live

3 **Idolatry** The Sin Beneath The Sin

4 **Community** The Context For Change

5 **Witness** An Alternate City

6 **Work** Cultivating The Garden

7 **Justice** A People For Others

8 **Eternity** The World That Is To Come

The study guide contains Bible studies, discussion questions on the DVD, and home studies. The home studies consist of a series of readings, quotations, exercises, questions, and projects to help delve deeper into the topic of each session. The guide also includes an extensive section of notes to help leaders prepare.

Gospel in Life Study Guide: 978-0-310-32891-9
Gospel in Life DVD: 978-0-310-39901-8

AVAILABLE ONLINE OR AT YOUR FAVORITE BOOKSTORE!

www.redeemercitytocity.com
www.gospelinlife.com

TWO SONS, ONE WHO KEPT THE RULES RELIGIOUSLY AND ONE WHO BROKE THEM ALL. ONE FATHER WHO LOVED BOTH LOST SONS BEYOND ANYTHING THEY COULD IMAGINE.

The Prodigal God curriculum kit contains everything that your church needs to experience a six-week preaching and small group campaign.

In this compelling film and study, pastor and *New York Times* bestselling author Timothy Keller opens your eyes to the powerful message of Jesus' best-known—and least understood—parable: The Parable of the Prodigal Son.

Dr. Keller helps you and your small group or church glean insights from each of the characters in Jesus' parable; the irreligious younger son, the moralistic elder son, and the father who lavishes love on both.

SESSION TITLES:

1. The Parable
2. The People Around Jesus
3. The Two Lost Sons
4. The Elder Brother
5. The True Elder Brother
6. The Feast of the Father

Session one contains the full 38-minute film. Each of the other five sessions will feature a short (2-3 minute) recap segment from the full length film to set up the small group discussion.

THE KIT CONTAINS ONE OF EACH OF THE FOLLOWING:

The Prodigal God DVD, *The Prodigal God* Discussion Guide, *The Prodigal God* hardcover book, and "Getting Started Guide." *Mixed Media Set 978-0-310-32075-3*

ALSO AVAILABLE:

Discussion Guide *(purchase one for each group member) 978-0-310-32536-9*

DVD *(purchase one for each group) 978-0-310-32535-2*

Hardcover book *(available in case lots of 24 only) 978-0-310-32697-7*